Shallow Well Church
1220 Broadway Road
Sanford, NC 27332

The Loving Heart

INSPIRATIONAL THOUGHTS FOR WOMEN

by Roy Lessin

Presented to: _____

From: _____

Date: _____

A Division of The AIM Group, Inc.
Franklin, TN
© 2005 The AIM Group, Inc.
Text Copyright © 2005 Roy Lessin
Original Artwork © 2005 Mary Leonard
All Rights Reserved
Printed in China
www.penmanpaper.com

Scripture is from the Holman Christian Standard Bible

The Loving Heart

INSPIRATIONAL THOUGHTS FOR WOMEN

by Roy Lessin

"God created man in His own image;
He created him in the image of God;
He created them male and female."

Genesis 1:27

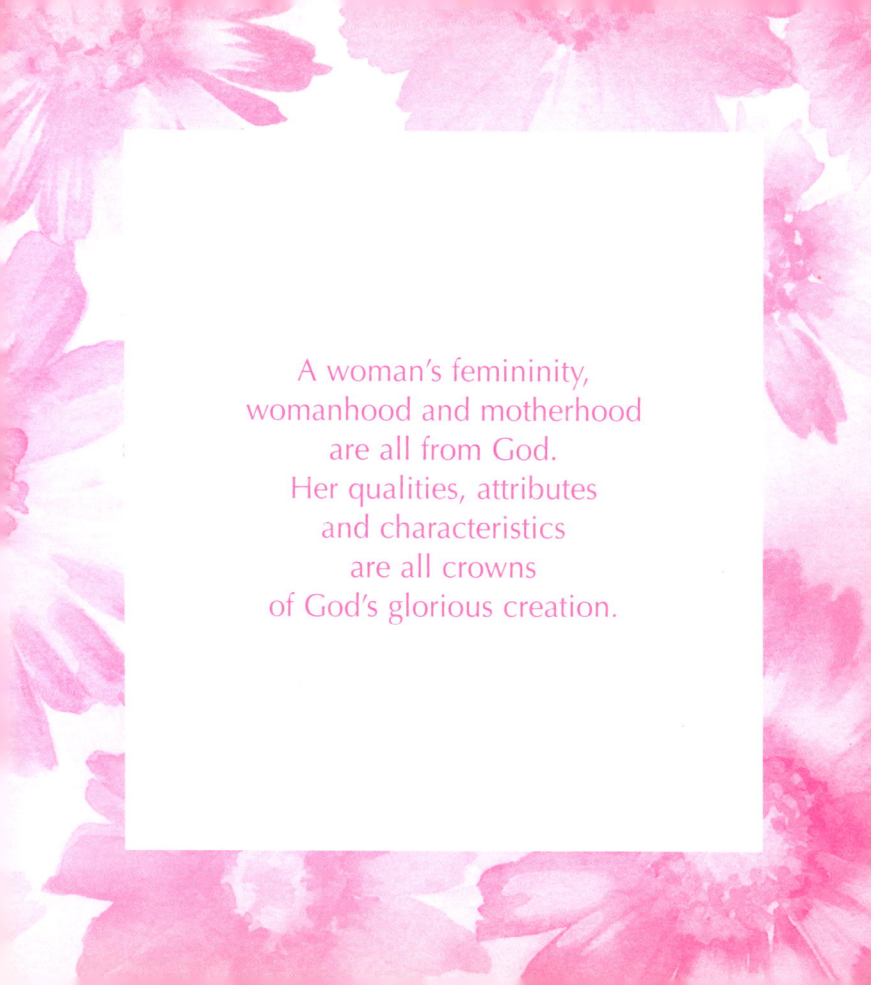

A woman's femininity,
womanhood and motherhood
are all from God.
Her qualities, attributes
and characteristics
are all crowns
of God's glorious creation.

For it was You who created my inward parts;
You knit me together in my mother's womb. I will
praise You, because I have been
remarkably and wonderfully made.
Your works are wonderful,
and I know [this] very well.

My bones were not hidden from You
when I was made in secret,
when I was formed
in the depths of the earth.

Your eyes saw me when I was formless;
all [my] days were written
in Your book and planned
before a single one of them began.

Psalm 139:13-16

God created a woman's heart
to be a unique
and caring reflection of His heart.

Through her touch, her tears,
and her tenderness
we have a deeper insight
into the compassion of God.

A woman's beauty is so much more
than what is seen with our eyes.
It is her inner life...
the radiating warmth of the Spirit's fire,
the sweet fragrance of the Father's joy,
the profound quietness of a heart
that trusts Jesus.

Gwen Faulkenberry

But You, Lord, are a compassionate
and gracious God, slow to anger
and abundant in faithful love and truth.

Psalm 86:15

Through a woman's words, ways,
and wisdom we have
a richer understanding
of the nurturing of God.

The Lord will always lead you,
satisfy you in a parched land,
and strengthen your bones.
You will be like a watered garden
and like a spring whose waters
never run dry.

Isaiah 58:11

Through a woman's insight,
inventiveness, and intuition
we have a greater appreciation
of the creativity of God.

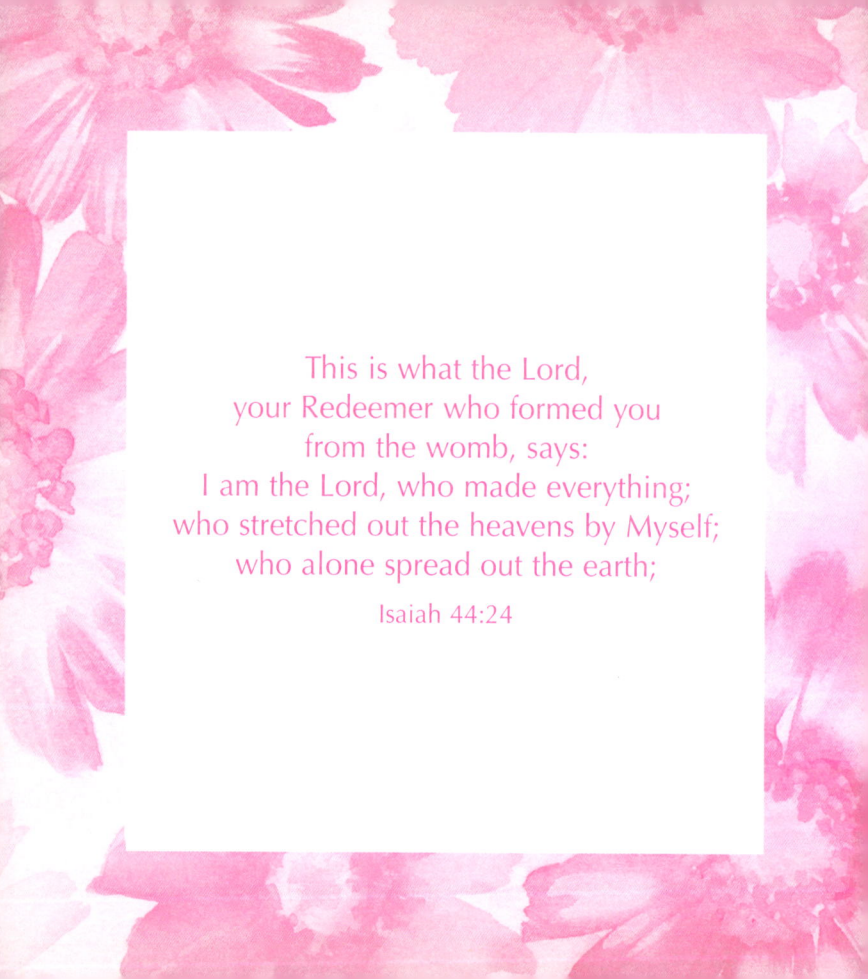

This is what the Lord,
your Redeemer who formed you
from the womb, says:
I am the Lord, who made everything;
who stretched out the heavens by Myself;
who alone spread out the earth;

Isaiah 44:24

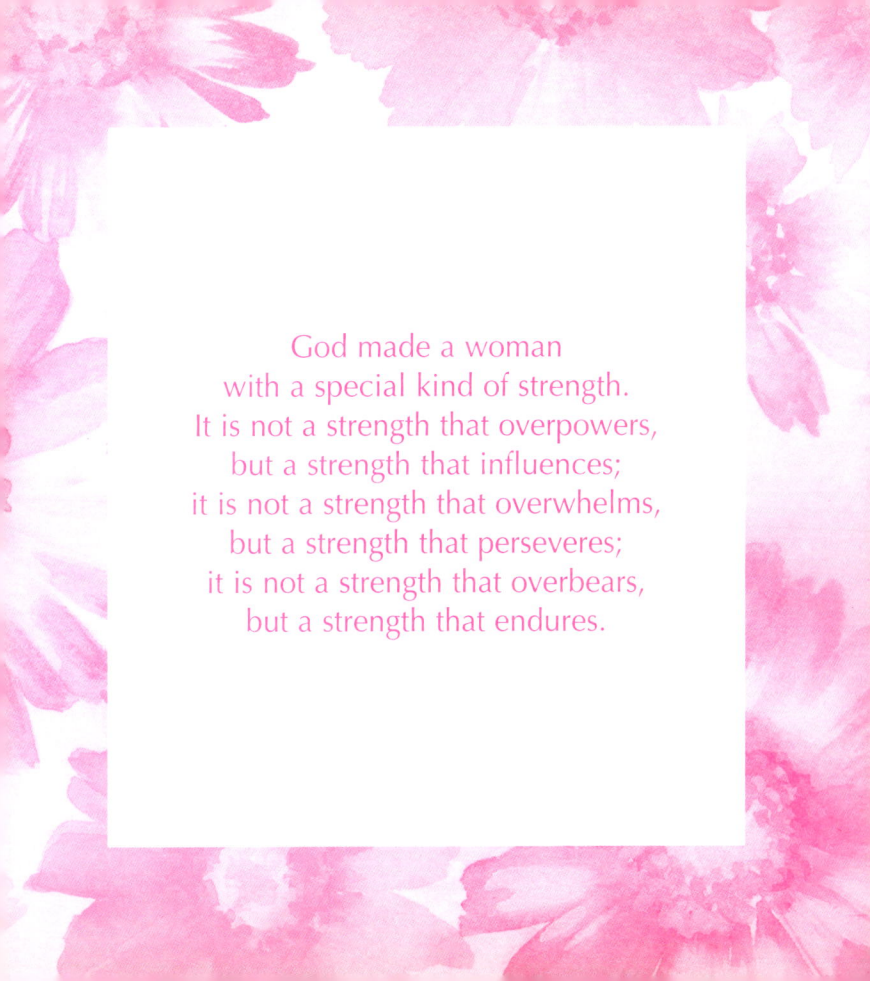

God made a woman
with a special kind of strength.
It is not a strength that overpowers,
but a strength that influences;
it is not a strength that overwhelms,
but a strength that perseveres;
it is not a strength that overbears,
but a strength that endures.

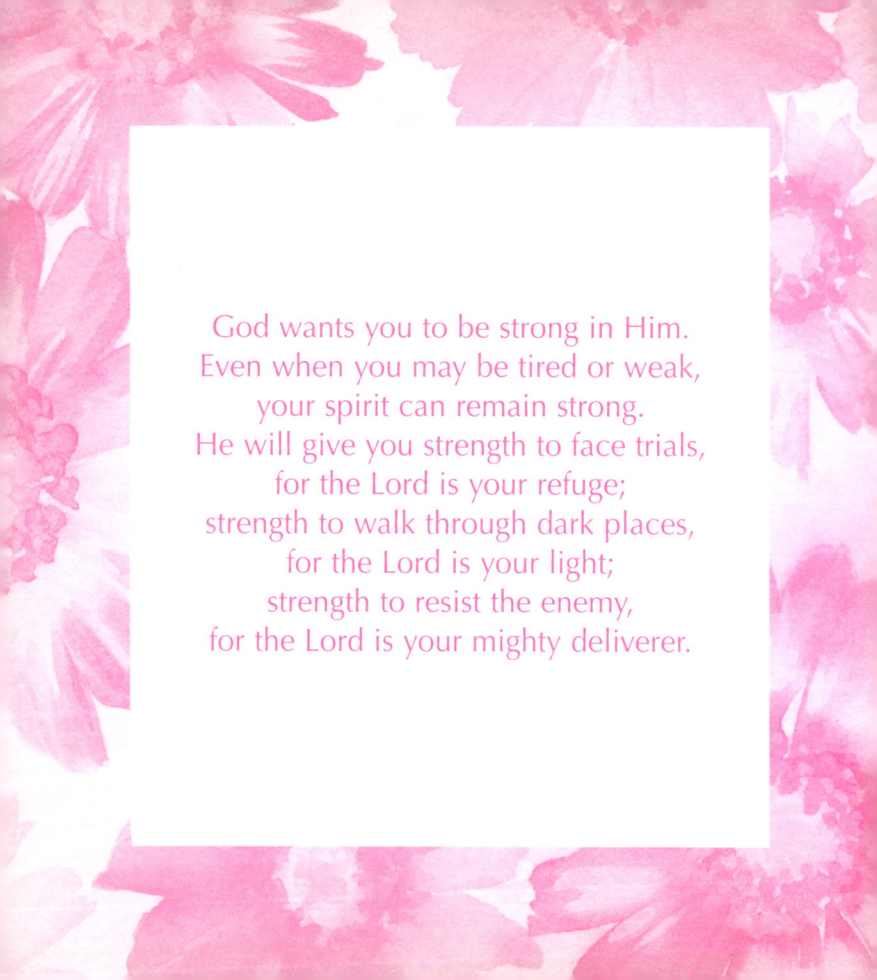

God wants you to be strong in Him.
Even when you may be tired or weak,
your spirit can remain strong.
He will give you strength to face trials,
for the Lord is your refuge;
strength to walk through dark places,
for the Lord is your light;
strength to resist the enemy,
for the Lord is your mighty deliverer.

...your strength will lie in quiet confidence.
Isaiah 30:15

Your heart can depend
totally upon the Lord,
for His strength never weakens,
His might never diminishes,
and His power never fades.

...be strengthened by the Lord
and by His vast strength.

Ephesians 6:10

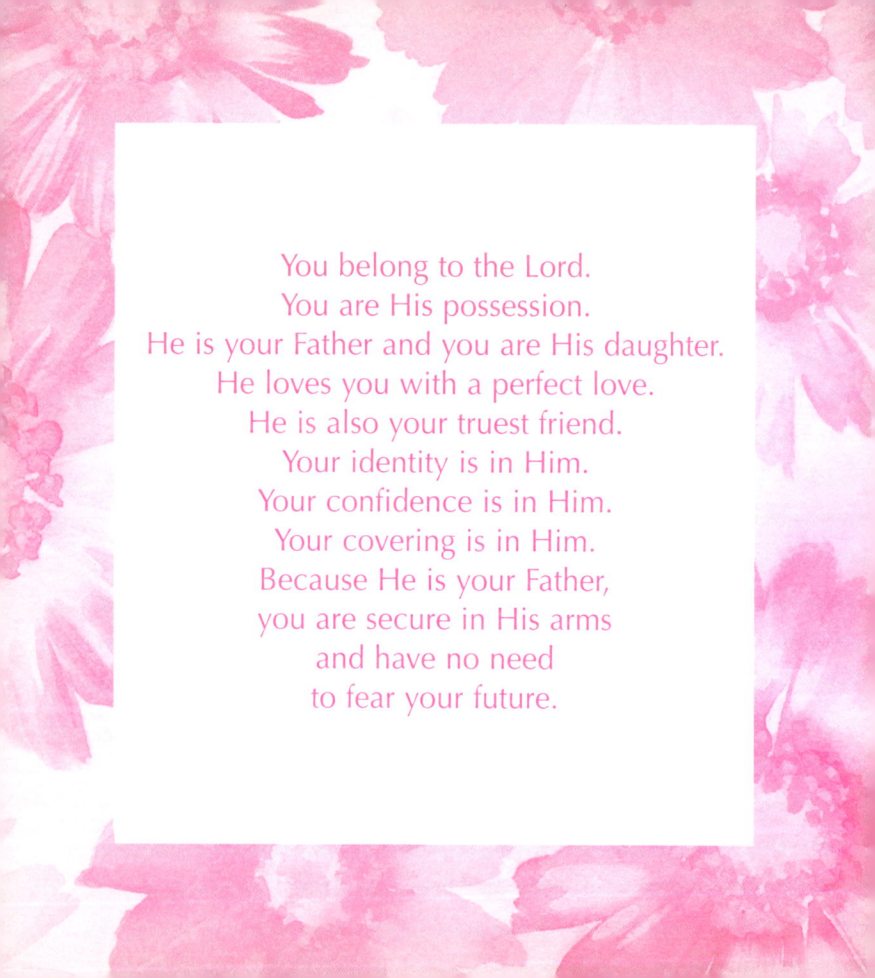

You belong to the Lord.
You are His possession.
He is your Father and you are His daughter.
He loves you with a perfect love.
He is also your truest friend.
Your identity is in Him.
Your confidence is in Him.
Your covering is in Him.
Because He is your Father,
you are secure in His arms
and have no need
to fear your future.

Look at how great a love the Father
has given us, that we should be called
God's children. And we are!
The reason the world does not know us
is that it didn't know Him.
Dear friends, we are God's children now,
and what we will be
has not yet been revealed.
We know that when He appears,
we will be like Him,
because we will see Him as He is.

1 John 3:1-2

God has called you to be a woman
who rejoices in Him.
You can rejoice
because He watches over your life
and takes care of you.
You can rejoice
because He is the Peace within you,
the Covering over you,
the Shelter around you,
the Guard behind you,
and the Guide who goes before you.

The one who lives under the protection
of the Most High dwells
in the shadow of the Almighty.

I will say to the Lord, "My refuge and my
fortress, my God, in whom I trust."

He Himself will deliver you
from the hunter's net,
from the destructive plague.
He will cover you with His feathers;
you will take refuge under His wings.
His faithfulness will be a protective shield.

Psalm 91:1-4

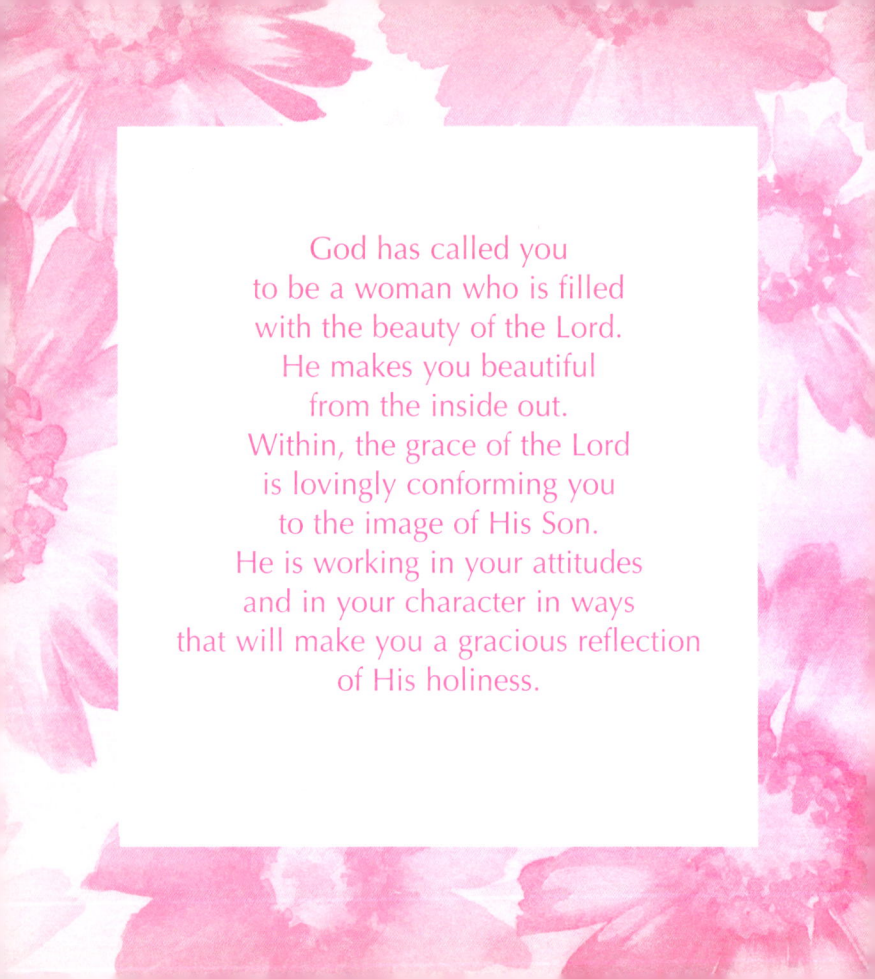

God has called you
to be a woman who is filled
with the beauty of the Lord.
He makes you beautiful
from the inside out.
Within, the grace of the Lord
is lovingly conforming you
to the image of His Son.
He is working in your attitudes
and in your character in ways
that will make you a gracious reflection
of His holiness.

Let the favor
of the Lord our God be on us...

Psalm 90:17

Worship the Lord
in the splendor of [His] holiness...

Psalm 96:9

A Woman's Prayer

Father, through my face
may your beauty shine,
through my voice
may your praise be heard,
through my hands
may your works be extended,
through my life
may your love be over all.

God Knows Your Heart

For every hectic day,
God is your quiet rest.
For every painful experience,
He is your healing touch.
For every disappointment,
He is your certain hope.
For every turbulent storm,
He is your calming peace.
For every hurtful action,
He is your forgiving love.

...a woman who fears the Lord will be praised.

Proverbs 31:30

God has called you
to be a woman
who trusts in the Lord
in all of your ways,
for all of your life,
with all of your heart.

Love never fails.
That is, it never tapers off or dies out.
Love never gets pulled off course
in its direction, or gets pushed off center
in its purpose. It will never be without effect.
It will never move away or turn away.
It can never be bought out
and will not sell out. Love will never wear out,
tire out, fade out, or cancel out.
It will never pull down, put down,
or pull away. It will never be useless,
inactive, or inattentive.
Love will never be inferior to anything.

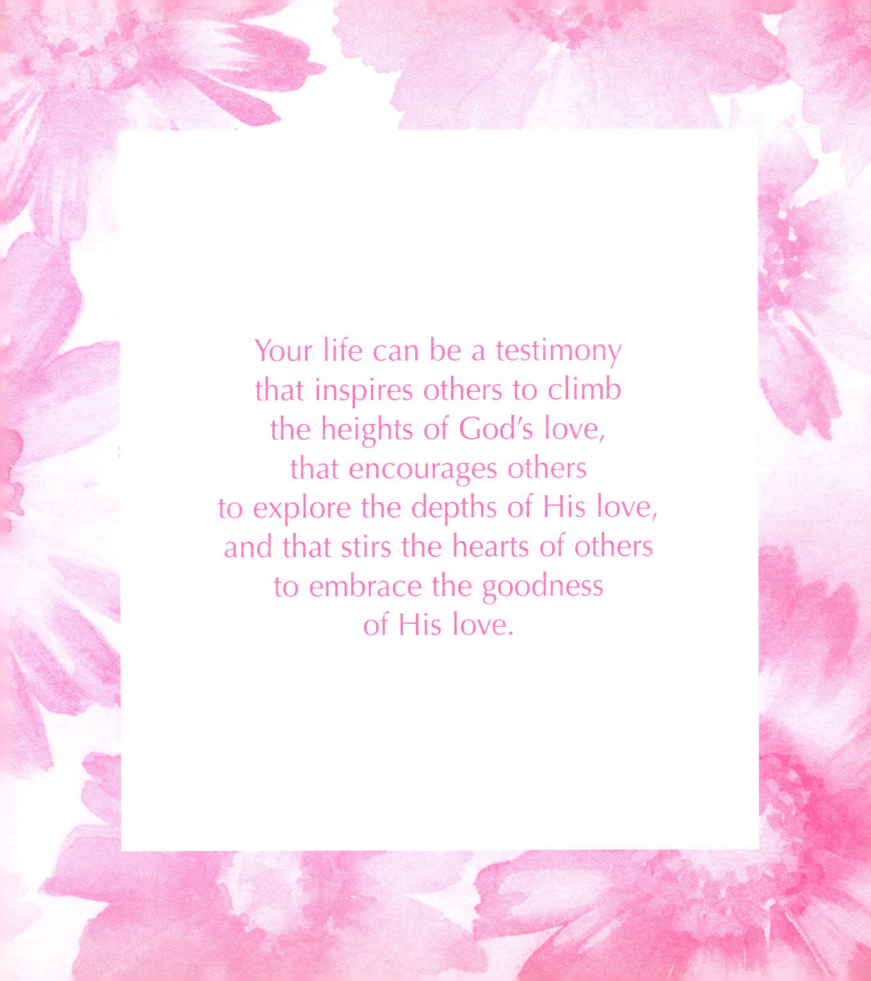

Your life can be a testimony
that inspires others to climb
the heights of God's love,
that encourages others
to explore the depths of His love,
and that stirs the hearts of others
to embrace the goodness
of His love.

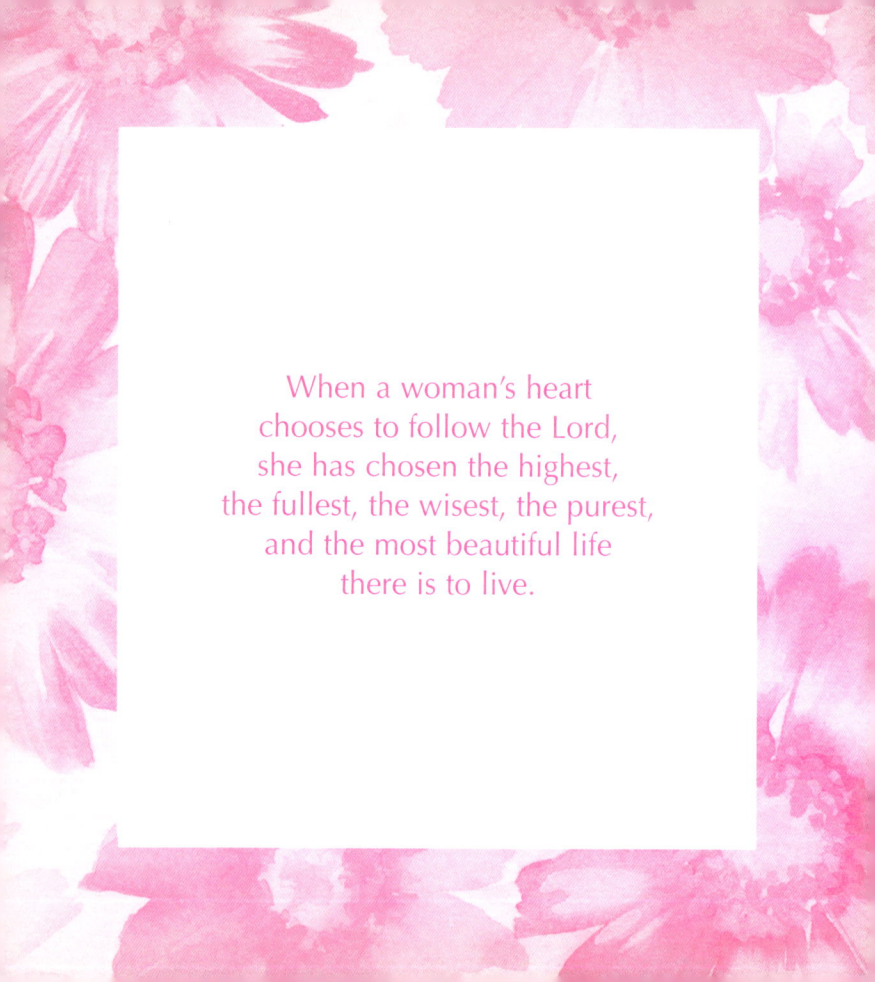

When a woman's heart
chooses to follow the Lord,
she has chosen the highest,
the fullest, the wisest, the purest,
and the most beautiful life
there is to live.

Seek the Lord in your hunger,
for He is your bread;
seek Him in your thirst,
for He is the Living Water;
seek Him in your need,
for He is your Provider.

Seek Him in openness,
in brokenness, in truth,
and in faith.

Seek Him, for He is
your exceeding great reward.

For our hearts rejoice in Him,
because we trust in His holy name.

Psalm 33:21

A mother is praised
for the beauty her children
find within her –
precious jewels of the soul and spirit.
These are the riches
that only love can give
and only the heart can treasure.

Through a mother's heart
flows an endless river
of ceaseless love.

Blessed be the God
and Father of our Lord Jesus Christ,
the Father of mercies
and the God of all comfort.

2 Corinthians 1:3

Every child needs comfort.
In times of trouble, pain, or fear
a child looks
for a mother's outstretched arms.
In her arms,
a child is sheltered, reassured,
soothed, and quieted.

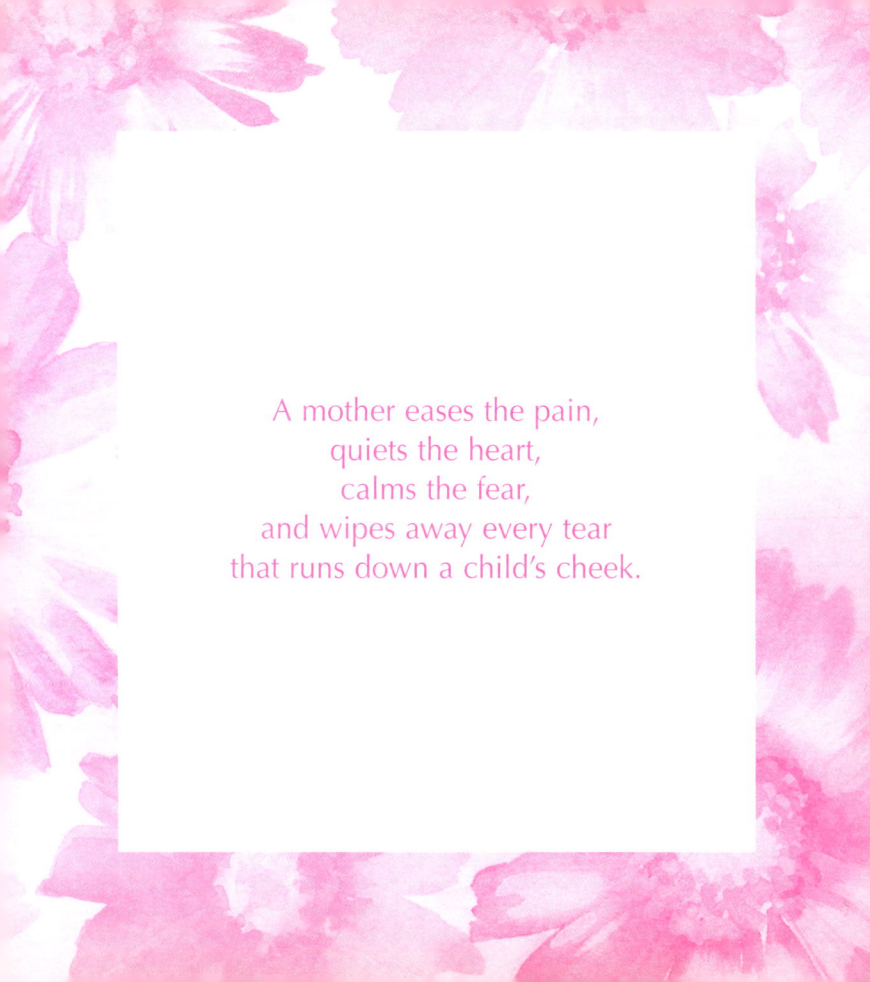

A mother eases the pain,
quiets the heart,
calms the fear,
and wipes away every tear
that runs down a child's cheek.

As a mother comforts her son,
so I will comfort you...

Isaiah 66:13

To comfort is to encourage.
A child hears many voices each day,
but no voice is as clear or as sweet
as his mother's voice.
A mother's voice rings true.
Her voice is the sound of belonging.
It speaks forth the child's name
as no other voice can do.

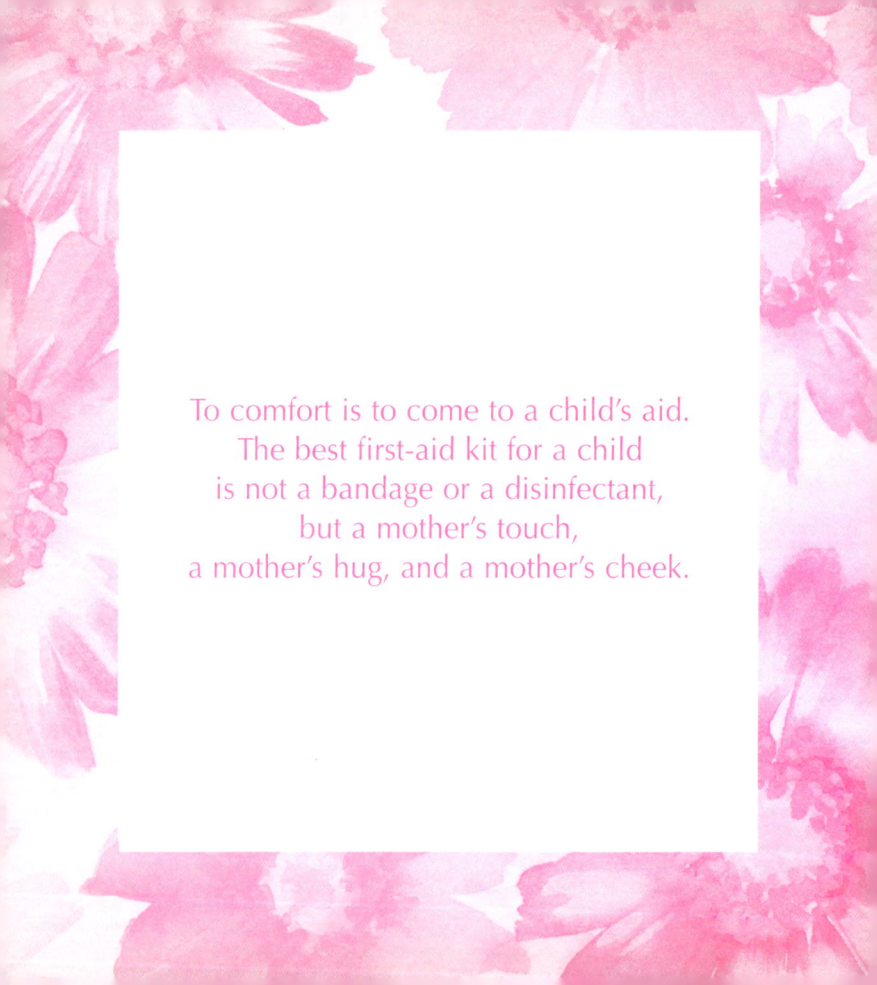

To comfort is to come to a child's aid.
The best first-aid kit for a child
is not a bandage or a disinfectant,
but a mother's touch,
a mother's hug, and a mother's cheek.

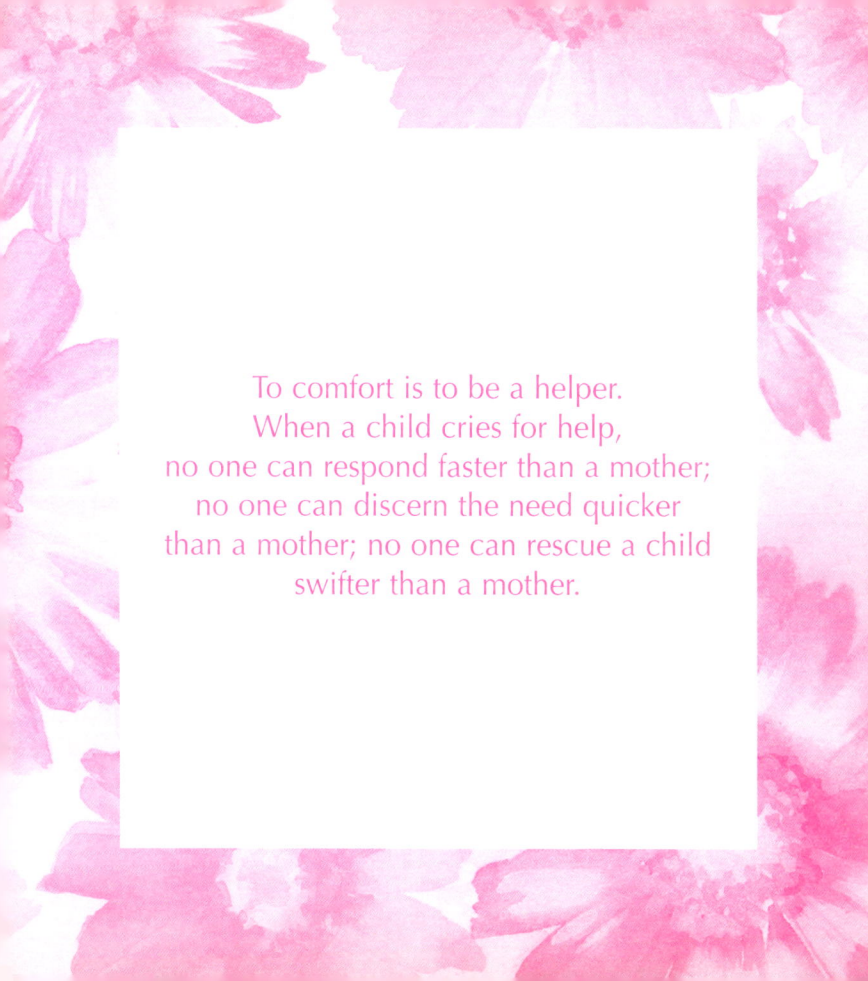

To comfort is to be a helper.
When a child cries for help,
no one can respond faster than a mother;
no one can discern the need quicker
than a mother; no one can rescue a child
swifter than a mother.

In my distress I called to the Lord,
and He answered me:
Out of the depths I call to You, Lord!
On the day I called, You answered me;
You increased strength within me.

Psalm 120:1, 130:1, 138:3

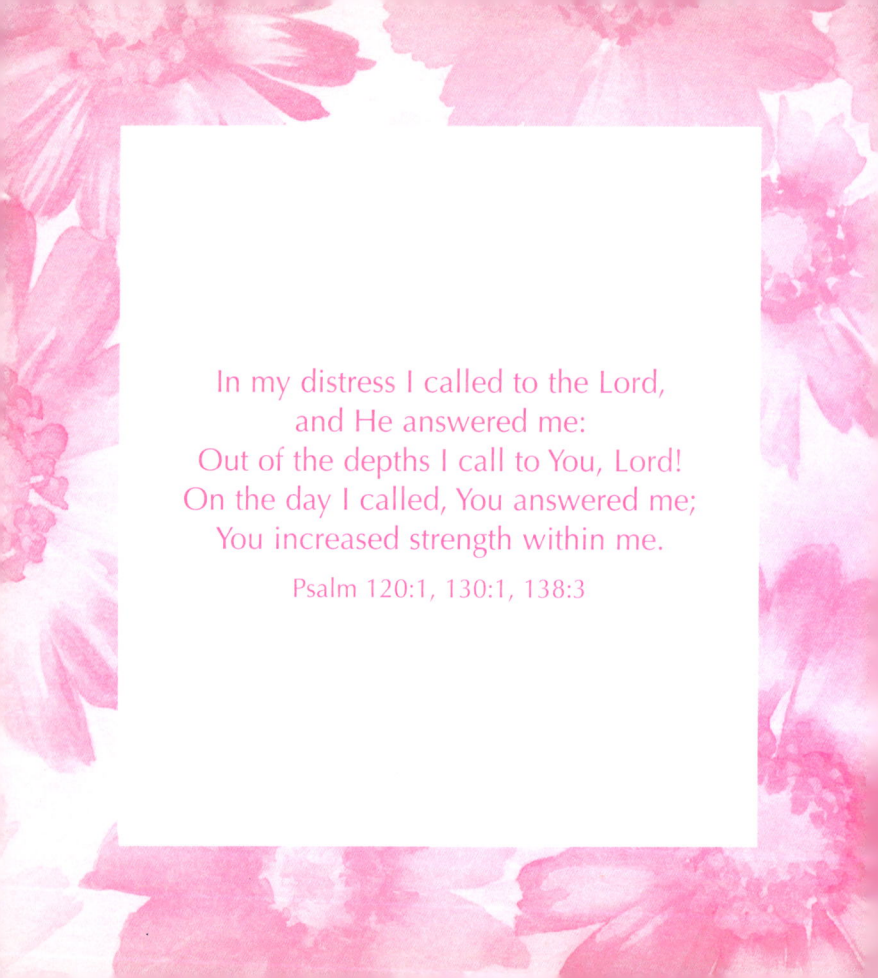

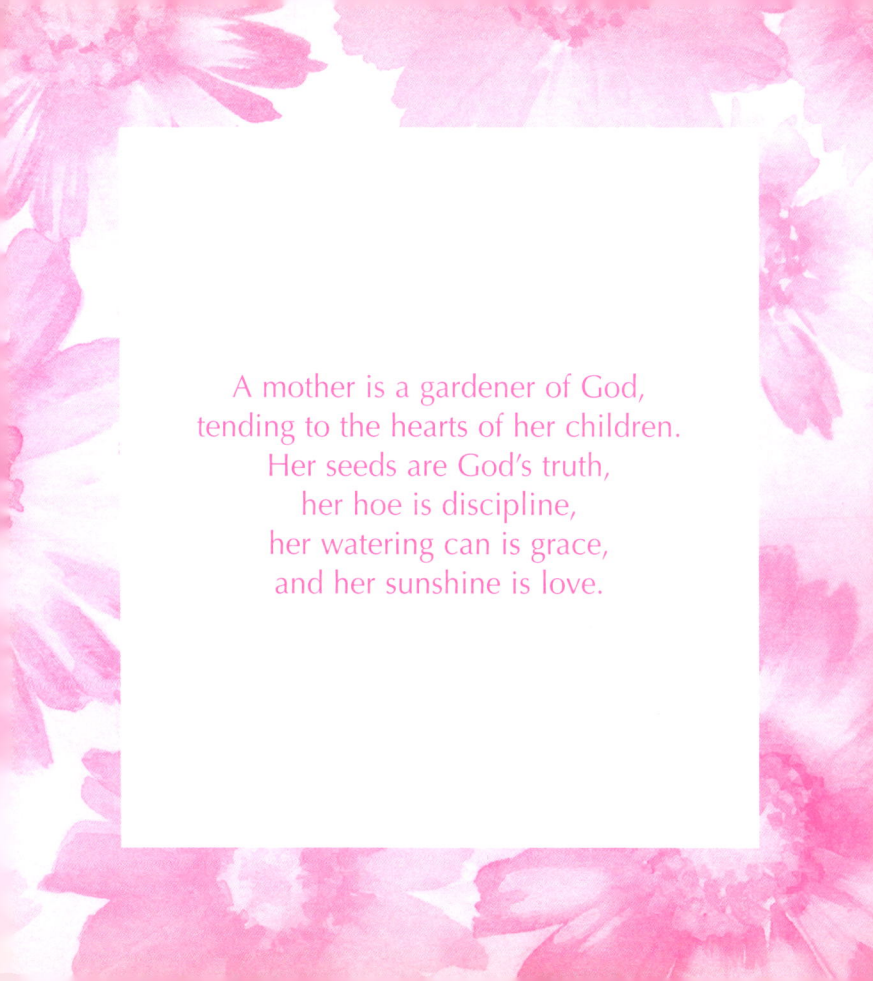

A mother is a gardener of God,
tending to the hearts of her children.
Her seeds are God's truth,
her hoe is discipline,
her watering can is grace,
and her sunshine is love.

When God made mothers
He formed within them
qualities of His own nature –
an unconditional love,
a watchful eye, a caring touch,
a listening ear, a protective hand,
a giving heart.

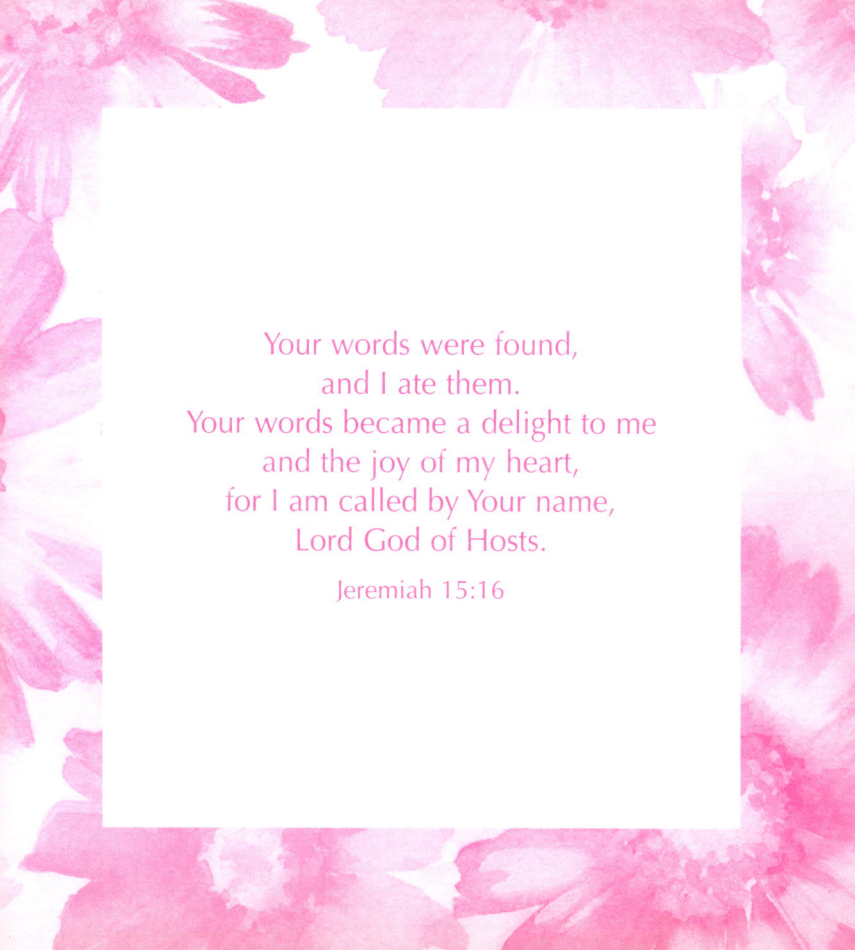

Your words were found,
and I ate them.
Your words became a delight to me
and the joy of my heart,
for I am called by Your name,
Lord God of Hosts.

Jeremiah 15:16

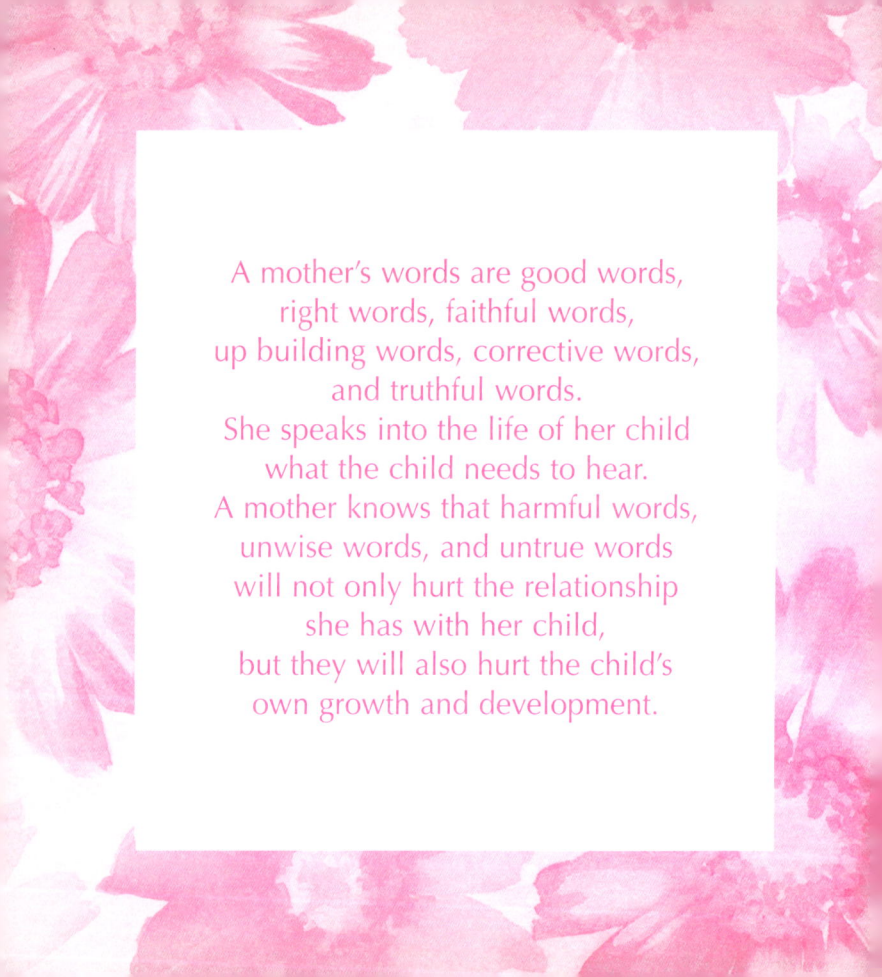

A mother's words are good words,
right words, faithful words,
up building words, corrective words,
and truthful words.
She speaks into the life of her child
what the child needs to hear.
A mother knows that harmful words,
unwise words, and untrue words
will not only hurt the relationship
she has with her child,
but they will also hurt the child's
own growth and development.

When a mother speaks truth to her child
she is speaking reality.
Truth is not pretend, make-believe, or fantasy.
When a mother speaks truth
she is speaking the heart of God
into the heart of her child.

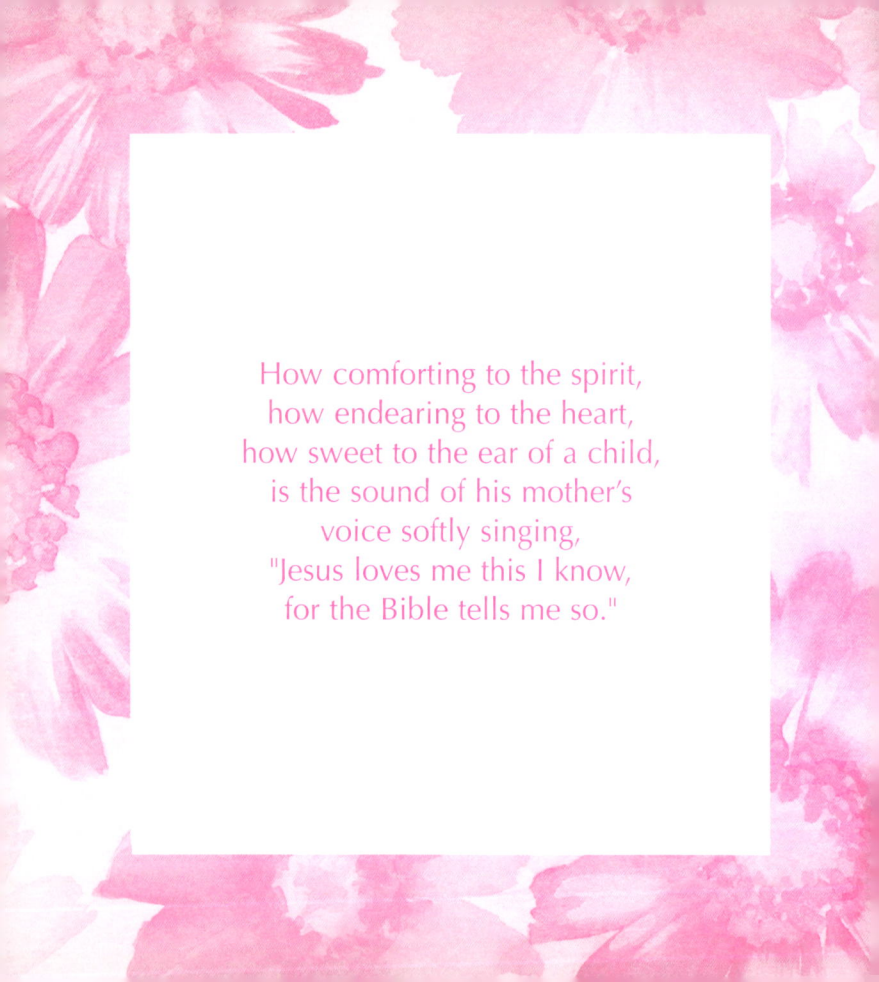

How comforting to the spirit,
how endearing to the heart,
how sweet to the ear of a child,
is the sound of his mother's
voice softly singing,
"Jesus loves me this I know,
for the Bible tells me so."

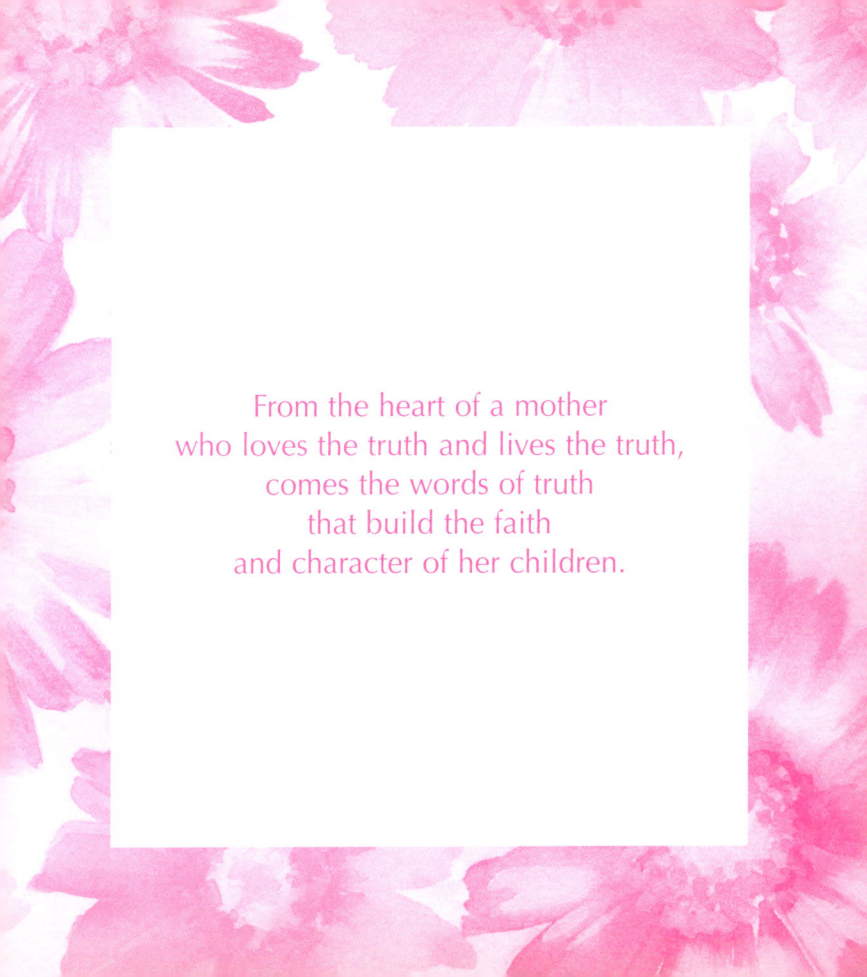

From the heart of a mother
who loves the truth and lives the truth,
comes the words of truth
that build the faith
and character of her children.

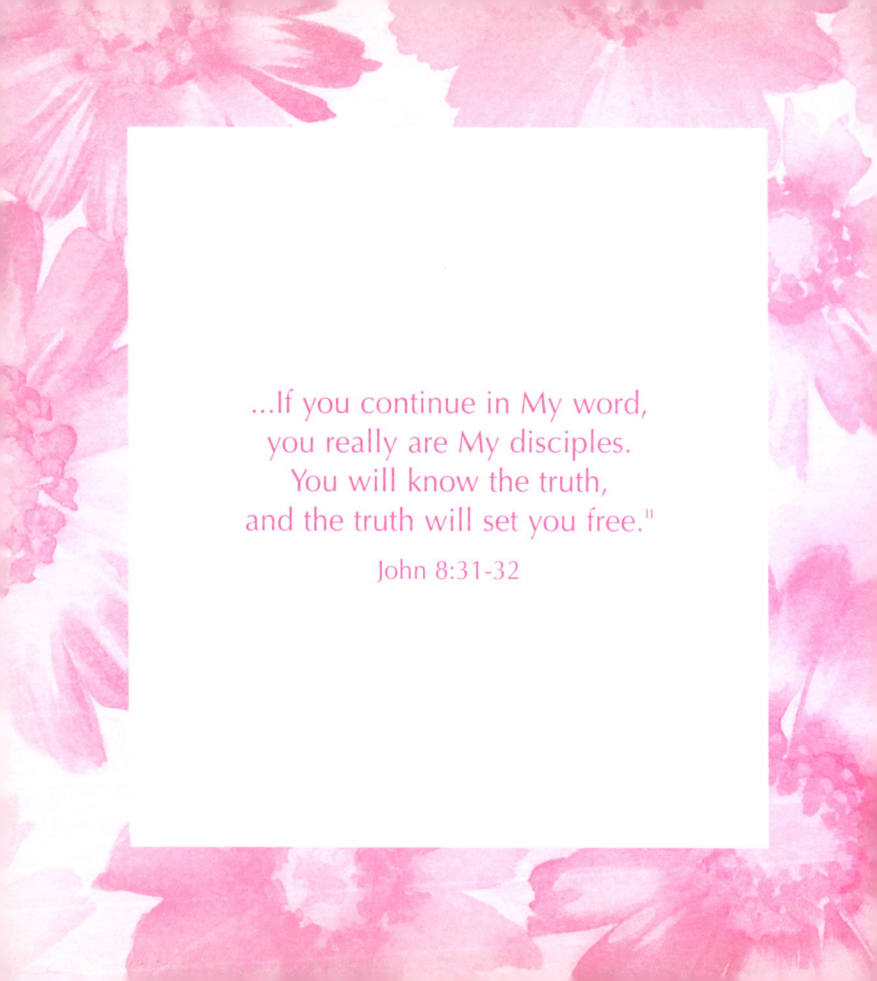

...If you continue in My word,
you really are My disciples.
You will know the truth,
and the truth will set you free."

John 8:31-32

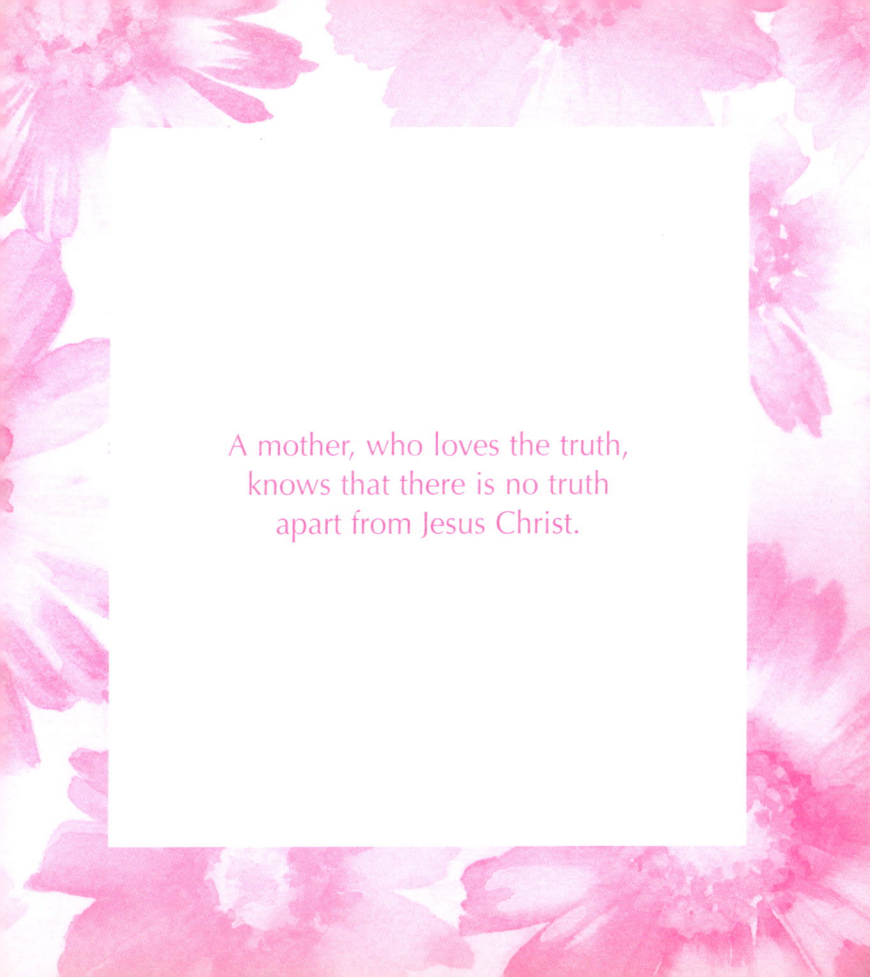

A mother, who loves the truth,
knows that there is no truth
apart from Jesus Christ.

Teach me Your way, Lord,
and I will live by Your truth.
Give me an undivided mind
to fear Your name.

Psalm 86:11

All virtue in a mother's life
and all integrity in her character
are rooted in the truth.
These precious qualities
make every mother truly beautiful.

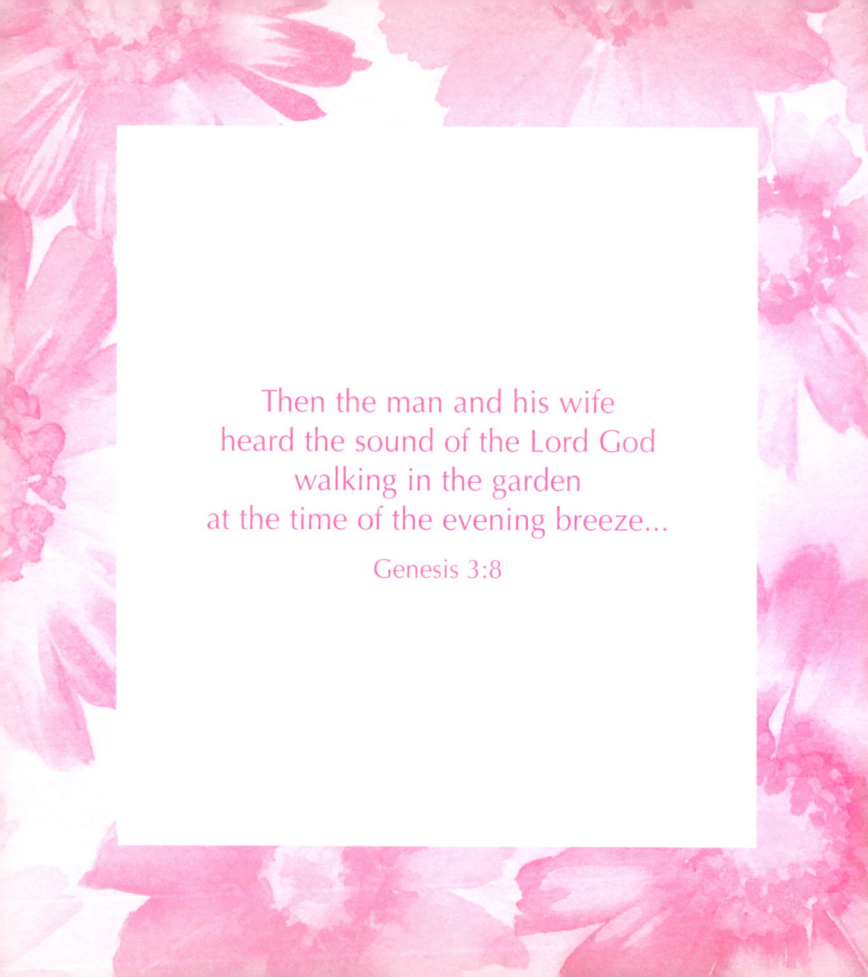

Then the man and his wife
heard the sound of the Lord God
walking in the garden
at the time of the evening breeze...

Genesis 3:8

It is believed that a child learns
to identify the voice of its mother
while it is still in her womb.
It is her voice that the child is drawn to
and responds to the soonest.
When a mother holds her newborn
and speaks sweet little words
into his or her ears, the child is comforted
because the ever-growing bond of love
between the mother and child
has already been established.

It has been said
that the sweetest words in our language are
"Mother, Home, and Heaven;"
and one might almost say the word home
included them all;
for who can think of home without
remembering the gentle mother
who sanctified it by her presence?
And is not home
the dearest name for heaven?
We think of that better land as a home
where brightness will never end in night...

...Oh, then, may our homes on earth
be the centers of all our joys;
may they be as green spots in the desert,
to which we can retire when weary
of the cares and perplexities of life,
and drink the clear waters of a love
which we know to be sincere
and always unfailing.

-Saturday Evening Post late 1800's issue.

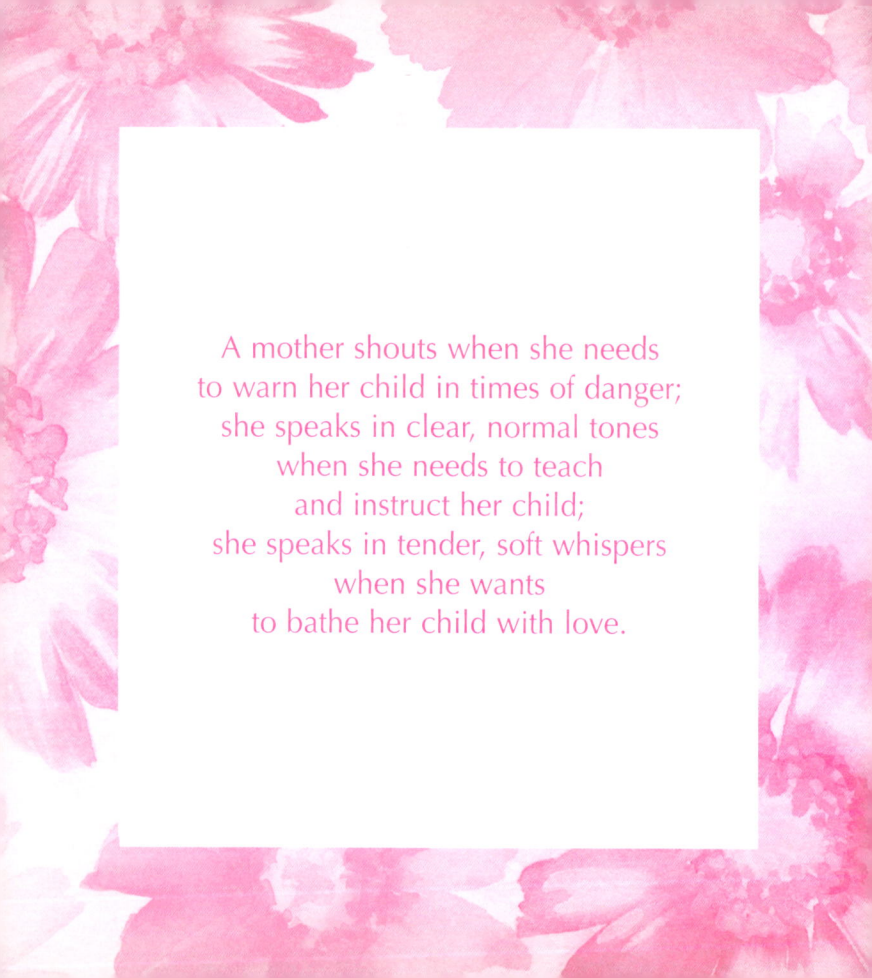

A mother shouts when she needs
to warn her child in times of danger;
she speaks in clear, normal tones
when she needs to teach
and instruct her child;
she speaks in tender, soft whispers
when she wants
to bathe her child with love.

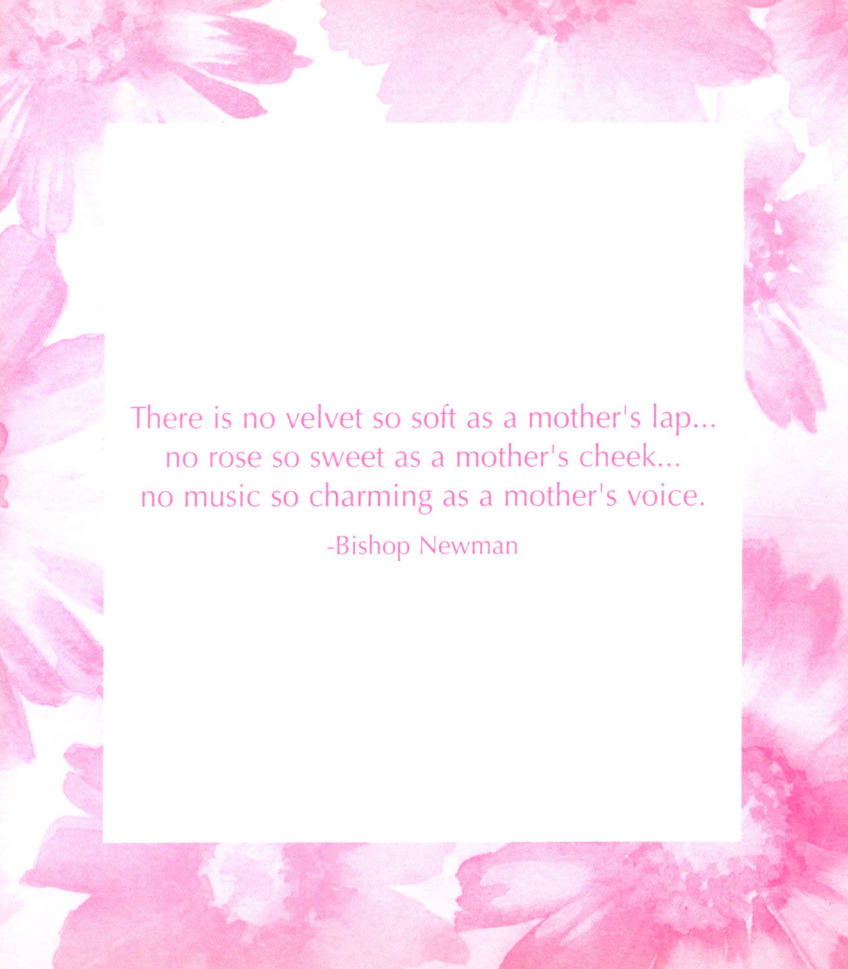

There is no velvet so soft as a mother's lap...
no rose so sweet as a mother's cheek...
no music so charming as a mother's voice.

-Bishop Newman

A mother is a child's number one fan and cheerleader.

I will instruct you
and show you the way to go;
with My eye on you,
I will give counsel.

Psalm 32:8

The heart of the mother
is the schoolroom of the child.

One mother is more
than a hundred schoolmasters.

- G. Wordsworth

A mother is the best teacher
a child can have.
She teaches by word and example,
in the early morning
and late at night,
and when it is convenient or inconvenient.
She is a teacher
who knows each child by heart.

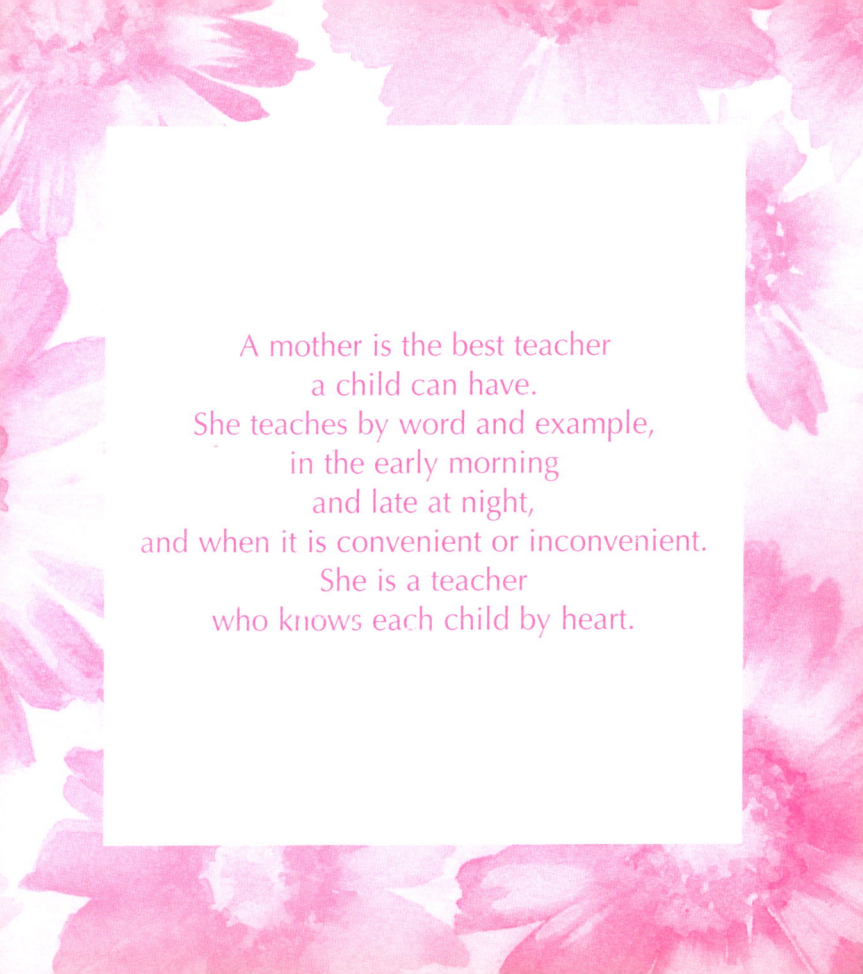

A house is built by wisdom,
and it is established by understanding;

Proverbs 24:3

She opens her mouth with wisdom,
and loving instruction is on her tongue.

Proverbs 31:26

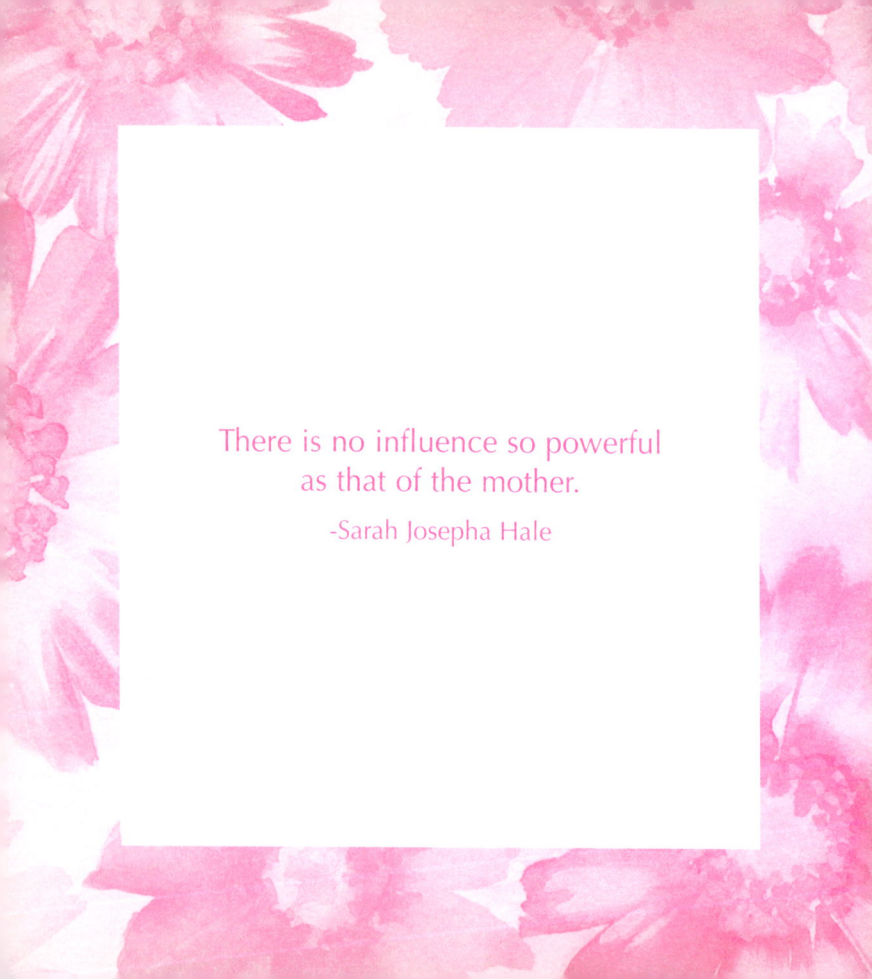

There is no influence so powerful
as that of the mother.

-Sarah Josepha Hale

All that I am or hope to be,
I owe to my mother.

-Abraham Lincoln

A mother's best teaching tools
are a peaceful spirit,
a graceful manner,
a gentle way,
and a contented heart.

A mother's teaching
impacts a child's mind,
influences a child's choices,
motivates a child's direction,
inspires a child's faith,
shapes a child's will,
and enlightens a child's heart.

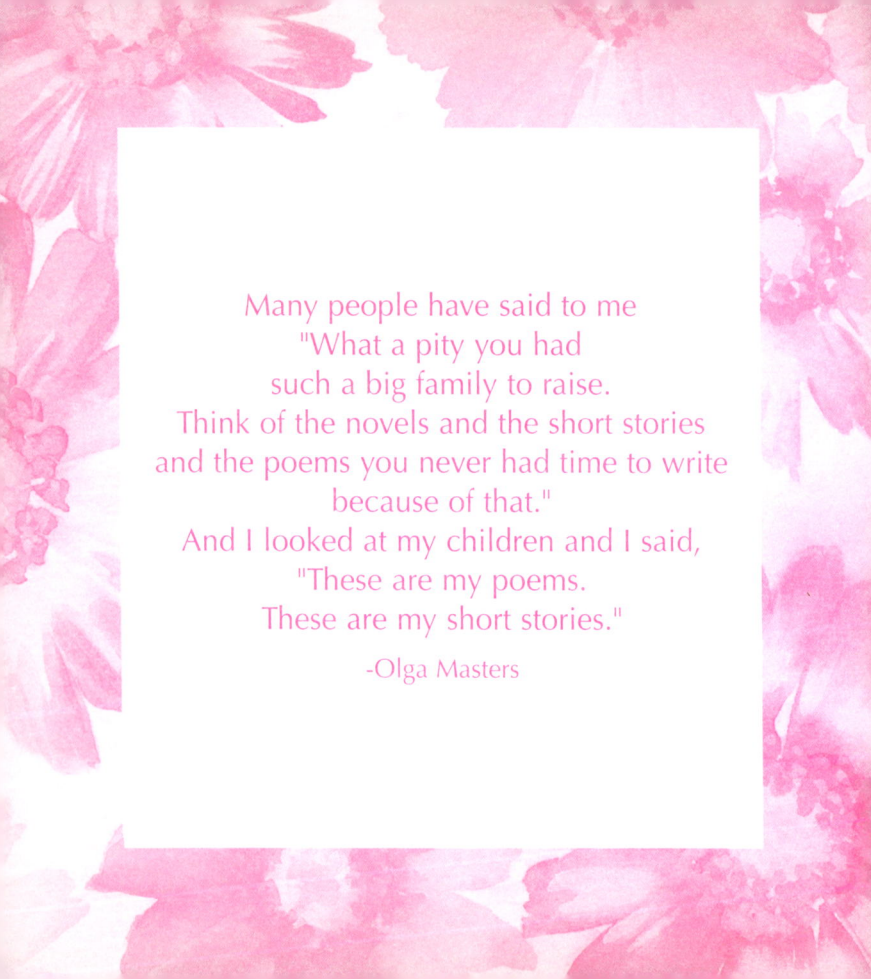

Many people have said to me
"What a pity you had
such a big family to raise.
Think of the novels and the short stories
and the poems you never had time to write
because of that."
And I looked at my children and I said,
"These are my poems.
These are my short stories."

-Olga Masters

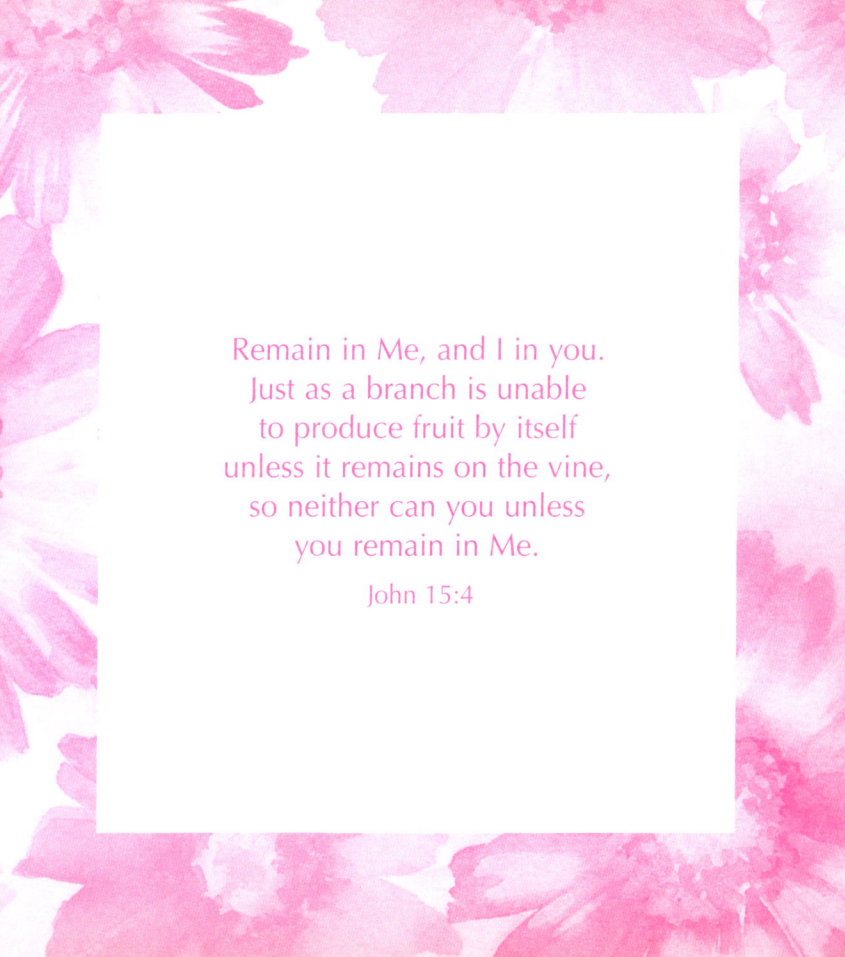

Remain in Me, and I in you.
Just as a branch is unable
to produce fruit by itself
unless it remains on the vine,
so neither can you unless
you remain in Me.

John 15:4

With heart and voice,
With hands and face,
No one can take a mother's place.

Children will always remain
in a mother's heart,
no matter how big they become
or how far away they move.

Children receive so much
from their mother's heart
because she gives so freely.

...God's love has been poured out
in our hearts through the Holy Spirit
who was given to us.

Romans 5:5

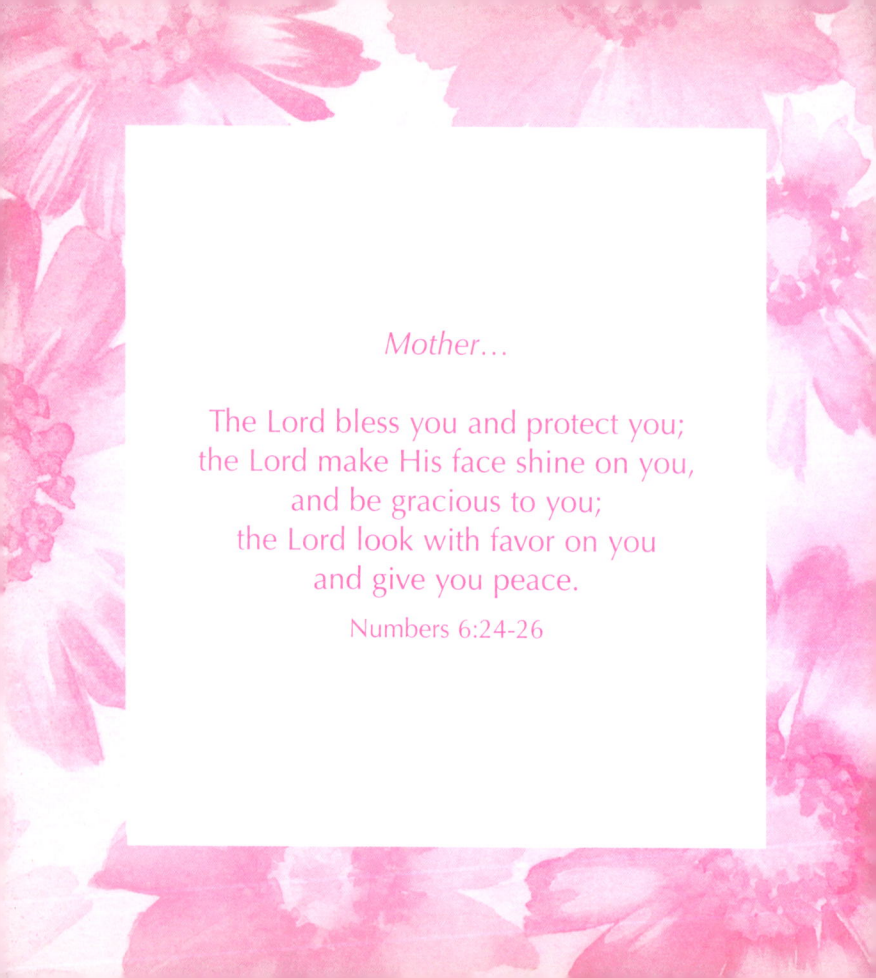

Mother…

The Lord bless you and protect you;
the Lord make His face shine on you,
and be gracious to you;
the Lord look with favor on you
and give you peace.

Numbers 6:24-26